HOW TO GET A

MEDICAL DEVICE SALES JOB

Your best resource to explains the
secrets of landing a career in the
lucrative medical device sales field

By: Daniel Riley

CONTENTS

Table of Contents

LESSON ONE: SALES PREPARATION

Every day, spectators watch professional athletes in amazement as they play a game. These athletes consistently perform and we watch them in awe. Professional athletes are well recognized as the finest individuals in their field. They are known to be the best of the best. However, few think about what it takes to reach this level of greatness.

For instance, have you ever watched a sporting event and thought about all of the off-season training that each athlete had to endure? Or have you looked at the individual driving by in the large luxury car and wondered about the hard work it took for them to earn it? In both cases it takes the same basic formula; preparation, devotion, hard work and precision execution.

To land a job as a medical device sales professional it takes the same ingredients. Ultimately, if you are really serious about working in medical device sales then you need to prepare for the job and devote yourself to obtaining it. After all, if they were really easy to get, everyone would have a job in this industry and it wouldn't be so special!

With this said, I can tell you from personal experience that the investment is worth it and these jobs are within reach. However, you need to know some of the secrets of the business.

Preparing for a medical device sales job is like preparing to enter the major leagues. If you want to make the big money, you need to prepare yourself accordingly. This means that you need to have a good understanding of the basic principles of sales.

To gain an understanding of sales, many people turn to written text. There are many books out there on selling and many of them are very good. I have read nearly all of them and one theme you will find in nearly all sales books is the concept of overcoming objections. What you ultimately need to do is put yourself in the shoes of the buyer and view the situation from their perspective. When you do this, it will become more evident of what is standing in the way of your objective.

You may have heard car sales people say; "What will it take for you to buy this car today" and may have thought, "Boy what a racket", but what they are trying to do (in a not so subtle way) is identify and overcome your objections so that they can make a sale. Simply put, they want to find out what is standing in the way of their sale.

To gain entry into medical device sales you have to do the same thing; Identify and overcome the objections of the medical device companies looking to hire people. This is necessary so you can make your first sale to them.

One of the basics is that understanding sales and feeling comfortable selling is absolutely mandatory for this field. After all, the title of your future role is <u>Sales</u> Representative. Working as a sales representative means dealing with people, products and of course competition. If you are not comfortable selling, you need to practice until such point that you are at ease with the process.

Take my word for it, if you aren't comfortable selling, you will never be able to sell yourself in the interview process. These companies are well-versed in hiring sales talent and your weakness will be flushed out during the initial meetings. So what you need to do is practice until such time that you are comfortable. Take every opportunity in your life to hone your sales skills. Whether it is selling an idea to a friend or negotiating for your favorite restaurant with a significant during date night. Whatever it is, keep fine tuning your skill. We will talk about sales experience more in Lesson Six.

Devotion is another essential ingredient to gain employment in the medical device industry. Just like a professional athlete devotes himself/herself to their sport, it is of critical importance that you devote yourself to finding a medical device sales job. If you are reading this book, you have already demonstrated that you are interested in obtaining this sort of position but do you have the passion and commitment to get it? As you probably know by now, securing one of these positions is not easily done. It takes a great deal of persistence as the competition is extremely heavy.

There is a good chance that if you are not devoted to getting the job then you will be bypassed by the person that is more committed. So this means that you need to commit to getting the job and apply what you learn in this book to get that edge you need to achieve your goal.

So let's talk about winning. In the process of seeking medical device sales employment you will ultimately have to win twice. First you have to make yourself stand out enough to get the job interview. Then you need to win during the interview process.

While you may not want to think about it, these jobs are highly sought after so your competition is notable. Thus, you need to find ways to differentiate yourself enough from all of the other candidates to get your foot in the door.

Second, you have to be ready to make your first big sale during the interview process. What you will ultimately win is one of the best jobs and careers available today.

What is interesting about your interview is that this is in many ways a sales call. The big difference is that YOU are the product. Selling yourself to the company recruiters and hiring managers is a critical step in moving forward. It will take preparation, positioning and professionalism just like selling any other product. We will talk more about these points throughout this book.

LESSON TWO: SOCIAL MEDIA

Social Media such as Facebook has been instrumental in keeping people connected with friends and family. You can come up to speed on someone's life in mere seconds making it a convenient tool for our fast paced society. It is unquestionably an extremely powerful and useful tool but also a tool that has to be managed properly.

Social media can be your friend or foe depending on how it is used. If you leverage social media strategically and avoid common pitfalls, you may find yourself steps ahead of many others trying to break into this business. If you do not pay attention to what your information says about you, you may be eliminated just as you are getting started.

Believe it or not, even if you are the perfect candidate for a position, you can lose the job well before you have ever had a chance to interview. Why you ask; because of what social media says about you.

Before you are contacted by any company, there is a very good chance that they have searched for your name on the internet to start gathering information. This is common practice by modern Human Resources so be forewarned.

It is estimated that nearly 86% of employers use some sort of social media in their search for employees and that number is growing by the day. Consequently, you need to ask yourself these questions;

- Do you think that a potential employer will like what they see about you?

- What messages are you sending out to the world?

- Are you aware of your "Personal Brand"?

To make sure that you are sending out the right messages about yourself, it is imperative that you objectively consider your "Personal Electronic Brand". This is probably a new concept for you so let me tell you what it meant by this term. *Personal electronic brand* is the combination of messages (either intentional or unintentional) that you are sending out to the world on your social and/or professional web-sites. It is much like your own advertising campaign for all to read that allows them to form an opinion about you.

Step back for a second and ask yourself these simple questions;

- What does my personal electronic brand say about me?
- What is my Facebook page saying about me?
- If I were looking to hire this person, how would I feel about them based on the information available on the World Wide Web?

If you don't like your answer then you need to immediately start doing some damage control. For instance, if there are pictures of you on your site that are unflattering or even risqué, you need to remove them right away. Pictures speak a thousand words and you can be very quickly disqualified if your pictures are sending the wrong message.

Have you ever heard the saying, "You can judge a person by the company they keep"? This saying applies to this situation too. Thus, if your friends or companions are negatively affecting your personal electronic brand then you must find a way to minimize the impact.

If you haven't used a social media site in a while, keep in mind that the internet never forgets! A Facebook page that you maintained in high school, college or any other time in your life can actually prevent you from landing the job you want today. While it may have been acceptable or fun at a particular time in your life, it may not be appropriate now given what you want to accomplish.

Thus you need to cleanse your on-line brand to ensure you put your best foot forward. Putting your best foot forward is ultimately what it boils down to; All of this effort is aimed at making a good first impression on your potential employer and preventing yourself from being eliminated before you get a chance to show them how great you really are.

So now that you removed the questionable or objectionable material, you want to create something that will entice the medical device employers. Ultimately, you want to make the best possible impression to peak their interest so that really desire to talk to you. Consider creating a front page that is professional and flattering (or at the very least, non-offensive). If you cannot do this for one reason or another, then keep the access to your pages private during your pursuit of this type of job.

One thing that you do not want to keep private is your LinkedIn page. If you are not already using LinkedIn you will want to start now. LinkedIn is effectively a virtual networking tool. It is similar to Facebook but with a professional focus. Consider it a professional networking site with the added benefit of allowing you to display your resume and brag sheet to everyone in the world. It is the perfect place to start shaping your personal electronic brand.

You should assume that all medical device employers that are interested in you will do a quick LinkedIn search on your name prior to speaking with you. This is good news for you as it presents you with an opportunity to start influencing the interview process at an early stage.

You want to create a page that really stands out. Create a page that grabs their attention and makes them want to talk to you. Make it a page that gets you the invitation to the interview process.

You don't have to put down everything about yourself but ensure that what you do put down is professional and compelling. Remember, first impressions really count and this could be the very first impression that Company X has of you.

If you are unsure about what you should put down on a social media page, search on the pages of others in the medical device sales industry and use them as benchmarks. Determine what you like and what you don't and create a hybrid page that uses all of the best practices that you have found.

Another interesting thing about social media is that it serves as a two way street. Not only can employers find information about you but you also have the power to leverage social media to your advantage to uncover information about your employers.

In many cases, social media will allow you to identify key contacts within the companies where you are seeking employment. By determining the name and employer of a potentially influential person within the medical device industry, you have already made an inroad. Even if you cannot send them an email, you can always send them a letter or leave them a voicemail introducing yourself. As you know, sometimes the hardest thing to do is get your foot in the door but social media can greatly assist you in this process.

LESSON THREE: PERSONALITY & PROFESSIONALISM

Have you ever met a person who had the type of personality that just made you cringe??? It is no surprise that a personality can make or break a candidate's chance of penetrating the medical device industry. Consequently, it is critical that you have adequate self awareness about your personality so you can correct any deficiencies and enhance your advantage.

The simple fact is that medical device companies are looking for individuals that will represent their companies well. After all, it is <u>you</u> that will be in front of their customers and it is you that customers will see as the company. There is a lot of money at stake for the medical device companies so they need to be sure that the people they are putting in front of their customers will represent the company appropriately. This means that the way you present yourself is of the utmost importance to the hiring companies.

It is absolutely vital that you conduct yourself in a way that they will find not only appropriate but also attractive. To be professionally attractive, you need to harbor the attributes that these manufacturers value. In fact, it is not that different than finding the perfect mate in your love life. You want someone that is compatible, attractive and maintains the characteristics that are important to you. Employers feel the same way and will not stop until they can find the best candidate possible.

While every employer is a little different, I have compiled a list of characteristics that can be considered universal in the medical device industry. Below are some highlights of what most medical device companies are looking for in a candidate.

Energy: Medical device companies want salespeople that are highly energetic. Energy is something that is attractive to both them and their customers. Energy is a key characteristic that is consistently desired by the medical device companies.

Think about a sloppy person moping around an office, classroom, or store that you can barely get out of a chair or lift a finger. Then think about the vibrant person that is full of energy, looking productive, and has a smile on their face. Which one do you prefer? And if you owned a business, which one would you hire?

You want to demonstrate a high level of enthusiasm for life and for the products that they sell. Now don't go crazy here and bounce off of the walls like a twelve year old full of too much caffeine, but you need to show some life and enthusiasm for the opportunity and for your career.

Attitude: A positive attitude is a characteristic that is critical in the medical device world. Medical device employers do not want people that have anything short of a "Can do" attitude. Negativity is not perceived well in this industry so you need to be positive.

During the interviews you will want to discuss positive things that happened in your life and/or career. If they ask you to talk about a negative event, eventually spin that story into a positive outcome. You absolutely do not want to come off as a complainer so even if there are negative situations that occurred in your personal or professional life, you will want to minimize them and focus on the silver lining.

Again, employers see you as a possible ambassador of their product and they want to know that your positive attitude and great outlook on life will be demonstrated to their customers.

Personality: The medical device industry is in the business of selling. They tend to do most of this selling through dynamic people. These companies don't want robots, they want real people with real personalities. The rationale for this is quite simple; It has been proven many times over that customers buy from people they like and connect with on a personal level. Consequently, you need to demonstrate that you are likable and you need to demonstrate your likable personality in every interaction with these companies.

Professionalism: Maintaining a professional demeanor is something that goes without saying but you would be surprised to learn just how many fail in this category. Professionalism is a broad term but it generally means dressing professionally, grooming professionally and most importantly, acting professionally in the world of business. This is truly a critical point so let's take some time and dive in a little deeper.

I recently had a newly graduated college student approach me about a job. He had a nice suit on, walked confidently and was well groomed. He was off to a good start but then he opened his mouth. In his initial dialog, he kept calling me "Dude" which continued throughout the conversation. What I could have told him is that he lost me at the first "Dude" but instead I politely listened to him until he was finished (I figured that I would at least get some great information on what not to do). After he finished I thought to myself that this "Dude" has a lot to learn about business.

So many high school and college graduates don't realize that their vernacular needs to change in the professional world. What has been cool or just the way you have spoken for years is no longer applicable in the business world.

If you are coming from high school or college, you need to leave the slang behind you. The business world does not use slang and that includes "Dude". It is up to you to conduct yourself professionally. The way you speak is of vital importance to hiring companies.

Choosing the right words is a very important part of sales. Salespeople are typically master crafters of sentences and it is of paramount importance that we can properly articulate our points. Our customers choose to buy or bypass our products based on our words and consequently it is imperative that the words we speak are carefully chosen to give us the advantage that we need to accomplish our goals.

This point cannot be reinforced enough as people of all ages and from many different backgrounds seem to get this wrong. Think about the way you speak and ask yourself these questions;

- Do you use a lot of slang?

- Do you think you sound professional?

If you use a lot of slang or don't sound like a professional then this is the time to change the way you speak or at least change it for all business interactions.

If you are unsure of whether or not you are projecting the proper outward appearance, a way to take an honest and objective look is by viewing yourself from a distance. Ask other professionals to give you open and honest feedback or perhaps video tape yourself having a business conversation. This will help you gain a better understanding of how the rest of the world perceives you.

Unless you are perfect, the chances are that there will be areas of improvement that you can make. However, before you can start making corrections, you need to know what attributes need to be corrected.

Self-awareness is so important in business. You need to constantly monitor yourself to make sure that you are sending out the right signals to the rest of the world. Always consider your attitude, professionalism, energy, personality, speech, etc. and look for ways to improve upon them. When you start to optimize these areas, you will find them to be handy tools that are always available to you to help you accomplish your goals.

LESSON FOUR: WHO DO YOU KNOW?

Building a network of contacts is an important part of business. In fact, a good number of medical device jobs are the result of effective networking within the industry.

Medical device sales people are magnets for other medical device jobs within the industry. Your objective is to meet these people and then leverage them. However, it is not just about meeting medical device sales professionals, it is about getting to know them and making a favorable impression on them so that they are willing to help you. You ultimately want to befriend them so they will be willing to be your eyes and ears. You want them to tell you when a job surfaces and be willing to happily recommend you.

Whenever you are interacting with someone in medical device sales, consider it an initial interview and act accordingly. It is of critical importance to not only make a great impression but also maintain a good relationship so that they feel absolutely confident in recommending you whenever they hear about a job opening.

I know what you are thinking; "Where am I going to meet medical sales representatives?" So let's take a step back. Your objective is to get to know as many medical device professionals as possible. The good news is that whether you know it or not, medical device representatives work all around you. Any of these people could hold the key to your future so if you want to enter the world of medical devices, it will benefit you to get to know these individuals.

There is not a single way to network and develop relationships with medical device sales people so you may need to be creative. The first logical step is to start looking at the professional circle around you. Perhaps you already know some of these professionals but didn't realize what they did for a living.

Another good way is to use alumni resources from your high school or college. The odds are in your favor that someone that graduated with you is now working in the medical device industry. Make contact with them and begin the process of building a relationship.

You want to meet and stay in touch with as many people in the industry as possible. The more people you know and stay in touch with, the greater chances you have of becoming aware of possible opportunities.

A popular and very efficient way of accomplishing this is through the previously mentioned social media networking sites. For instance, in business networking, LinkedIn is a very common networking site and is a good place to stay in touch. You can see updates by other professionals and stay up to date with the progression of professionals and companies.

Another way is to search for a medical device sales person either on a company's web-site, Facebook, LinkedIn, etc. that lives in your area. Once you find a name, you can then put together a compelling letter explaining that you are interested in entering their field and just want some advice. Ask for a short meeting perhaps over breakfast. Many sales people remember how hard it was getting their foot in the door so you will find that many sales representatives will be willing to help you.

Here is another secret; If you want to meet a lot of medical device sales people, attend the major medical conventions. Every industry has major conventions where physicians go to learn about the latest in their field of expertise. Most of the major medical device companies participate in these shows as sponsors so that they can show off their products to the physician market and build their relationships with their customers. This is also a perfect way to get your name out there.

The good news is that you don't have to be a member or physician to go to many of these shows. You can attend merely as a paying guest in many cases and can then begin the networking process in a very serious manner. Again, it is important to remember that you need to treat every interaction as an interview.

Also, be sure to let the world know what you are looking for. There are many medical device jobs out there that you may not have visibility to but someone in your social or professional network may very well have the key to your next opportunity. Make sure that everyone around you keeps their ears open for your dream job.

Once you begin meeting people in the business, you need to invest in and nurture the relationship. Just like any social relationship, business relationships often take a little time to develop. To give an example, I recently had a gentleman named Joe ask me for a job with my company. Joe and I went to the same college but I didn't know Joe very well during school and hadn't been in contact with him since graduation. Years after graduation, Joe contacted me through LinkedIn and immediately asked me to recommend him for a job. Needless to say I wasn't comfortable recommending someone for a job who I didn't know or haven't talked to in many years. However, if Joe would have stayed in touch over the years, things most likely would have been different.

The simple lesson here is that you need to stay in touch with individuals that you want to help you. Having a contact on LinkedIn is much different than having a friend or professional relationship with someone on LinkedIn.

LESSON FIVE: PREPARING YOUR RESUME

A resume alone will not win your dream job but it is an essential tool that you must have to achieve your goal. If prepared correctly, it should help you continue along your path.

It is no secret that medical device companies are inundated with the resumes of people that want to work for them. These resumes have a tendency to blend together so what you need to do is make certain that your resume stands out, is well thought out and, is constructed flawlessly, and is going to help you achieve your goal.

A good resume should capture the interest of the hiring company and increase your chances of getting hired.

Conversely, a poor resume is the quickest way to be eliminated from consideration.

There are many tips on the internet on writing good resumes and we could spend many hours discussing them but let's instead just look at some highlights. First, a resume needs to look aesthetically appealing. Before any employer looks at the content, they will see the overall layout. This layout will make one of three impressions; good, bad, or neutral. Obviously the objective is to try to make a good impression on your audience.

You want to invest some time into your resume to make sure that it is perfect. Be sure to be consistent in fonts, be concise in your wording, don't overcrowd the resume with too many details, don't go overboard with color and be sure to spell check. From an aesthetics standpoint alone, you want your resume to look appealing from a distance so that your resume stands out from the crowd and begs to be picked up and read.

Many college graduates ask me the same question; What should I put down as experience if I have never had a real job? The answer is anything you can think of that will work in your favor. This includes volunteering, internships, professional clubs, training, etc. This same concept holds true for parents that have taken time off to stay at home and raise children. Medical device companies want motivated and successful people. You ultimately want to look like someone that has been successful in whatever endeavors you have participated in as well as someone who has demonstrated a high level of motivation.

While it would be nice if you had experience in the exact field for which you are applying, employers don't necessarily expect that you have experience within their industry and with their product. They do however want someone who is professionally attractive. That simple piece of paper called a resume is your first (and possibly only) method of pleading your case.

Think about the experience that you have and find a way to tailor that experience towards the position. Maybe you have never had an official sales job but you were the top fundraiser for a charitable organization or for your children's school. Or perhaps you found ways to really excel in an academic activity that you participated in. Or maybe you helped the store you worked in reach their revenue targets. The key is to customize the experience so that it can be easily translated into sales experience by the person reading your resume.

If you have job experience, it is imperative to list some specific details and avoiding generalities. While employers don't need to hear about every detail, you need to avoid such general statements like "I performed well." If you were in sales for instance, put down some tangible numbers such as "Achieved 125% of quota for three consecutive years" or "Employee of the month five times". If you are coming right out of school, perhaps you were ranked second in your class or major.

One thing you don't have to worry about is stating an objective on your resume. Writing an objective is redundant as your application to a specific position indicates your objective. In addition, you have already stated your objective in your cover letter. Consequently, an objective on a resume just takes up precious space and adds to clutter.

Objectives belong on your cover letter and they should be written for the exact position you are applying. Again, you need to tailor your presentation for the audience so don't be tempted to recycle the same cover letter again and again.

It is also important to leave off all personal information besides contact information. Remember, this is a professional resume and not a personal biography. This may sound obvious but many people add erroneous items to their resumes that are irrelevant to employers.

Finally, print your resume on a high quality resume grade paper. A resume that is printed on cheap paper conveys the wrong message. A pack of quality paper is not expensive and it is not only a nice touch but it is somewhat expected these days. Quality paper sends a message to the reader that you made an additional investment. It also subconsciously associates your name with quality in the mind of the reader.

So many people fail to take the necessary time to invest in their resume. They see it only as a necessary chore. This mentality is great news for you as it will help eliminate some of your competition.

Create an outstanding resume and leverage this tool to make you stand out. After all, you have worked hard all of your life and this is the place to display this hard work and all of those accomplishments.

LESSON SIX: EXPERIENCE COUNTS

I know what you are thinking, how are you going to get experience in the medical device industry if you aren't given that first chance? The answer is simple, find a way to gain industry experience and knowledge through volunteering or any other way you can.

My phone is constantly ringing with medical device companies that want to recruit me away from my current employer. Companies and recruiters love experience and prefer to turn to people that can hit the ground running. This concept shouldn't be foreign to you as you probably do the same thing. For instance, when you hire someone to fix your house, do you hire a ten year old who has never touched a tool or a professional contractor? Or when you need to see the doctor, do you go to your friend who has no real knowledge or do you go to an MD? Even though we may not like to admit it, experience really does count. Consequently, the key is for you to find a way to get some sort of applicable experience on your resume.

Medical device sales is similar to many other sales jobs but with another category of a product and typically a more complex selling environment. A really nice thing about the field of sales is that many sales skills are directly transferable to other jobs. And since sales jobs are plentiful, there are many opportunities for you to acquire some experience.

Many of my colleagues started out in professional careers far different from where they are today. So what you need to do in your journey is find a sales job of any sort so that you have at least some sales experience on your resume. While it is preferable to have medical sales, this may not be possible when starting out. Just get solid sales experience selling insurance, paper, cars, clothing, etc. and do your very best to excel.

Once you have sales experience, you can find ways to parlay it into other sales jobs and start working towards the one you really want. I have seen this formula work many times over.

For example, just recently I coached a friend of mine and helped him move from selling copiers to insurance sales to medical sales. He simply followed this advice and used his contacts and sales experience to land a job with a medical device company. At the time he was hired by the medical device company, he had absolutely no medical device sales experience but did have a couple of sales positions on his resume to draw from which was enough to get his foot in the door.

The formula works but it takes an investment and persistence! After all, if getting these jobs was easy, everyone would be doing it.

LESSON SEVEN: BUILDING INDUSTRY KNOWLEDGE

Medical device sales representatives are heavily paid partly because the people in the industry have developed a sound understanding of the complex procedures and treatments. If you have ever worked in the medical industry you probably have found that many of the terms used make it seem like a different language altogether. Consequently, you need to do a little homework before you enter into the interviews so that you look prepared and can speak intelligently.

This is not to say you have to have the understanding of a physician but you need to know the basics and a little beyond. For instance, if you are interviewing for a dental sales position, research the company and product you will be representing. Understand why this product is used, frequent challenges, the market, competition, etc. If you do this you will substantially increase your chances of having a successful interview and outcome. This is especially true since so many people go to interviews and just hope for the best. Preparing yourself will help you shape your destiny as opposed to just hoping it will occur.

While this preparation takes a little more work on your part, think of how much time and energy you invested to just get the interview. You have made it this far, you have to go the extra mile to do everything in your power to advance yourself down the hiring process.

Here is some additional motivation; If you get to the point where a company is taking the time to either sit down with you or have a conference call with you, then you are well within reach of getting the job. Companies don't have the time or resources to arbitrarily interview candidates.

They sift through the resumes and applicants and interview a select few. You cannot let several hours of preparation come in between you and your dream.

Here is a real life example. The last interview I conducted on behalf of my medical device employer was with three candidates. All three were experienced in some form of sales, all three worked in the industry in some capacity and all three seemed similar on paper. So our company decided to find ways to differentiate the three by asking them basic questions about the industry. Only one of the three candidates had taken any time at all to prepare for these types of questions. The other two looked confused, intimidated and unprepared. Which one do you think we ultimately selected?

In a competitive field like medical device sales, knowing about the business and industry is something that is expected by the employers. However, it is surprising how many people skip this step.

By doing some industry research and preparation, you demonstrate motivation, a passion for the position and product, and even a courtesy to the people with whom you are meeting. After all, these companies have taken the time to learn about you, it is only fair that you took the time to learn a little about them.

LESSON EIGHT: WHERE ARE ALL THE JOBS?!?!?

When I was embarking on the same journey that you are pursuing, I had no idea where I should turn to find job opportunities. I found that most of these jobs aren't posted in the paper or even major job boards. However, the jobs are out there if you know where to look.

Besides using your network, the next place to search is the most obvious. If you have a particular company that you would like to pursue, go directly to their web-site. All of the job openings should be posted and you can apply on the site.

However, many candidates don't necessarily have a particular company in mind but instead just want a job in the medical device industry with a company that is willing to take a chance on them. What insiders know is that many companies that you have never heard of before are looking to hire people all across the world. These companies aren't necessarily household names but they need people and make hiring decisions daily. Thus, you need to know where to look to connect with them.

So where do medical device sales people turn when they are looking for a job? There are two good places to source these jobs. The first are medical specific employment sites and the second are medical specific headhunters.

You may have already looked to the internet for a job. Besides the obvious sites, there are several lesser known sites that are gold mines for medical device sales job postings. Have you ever heard of www.medreps.com? If you haven't, this site lists many medical device sales jobs that you would probably never hear of from any other source. There are many companies out there that you may have or may not have any familiarity with that looking for representatives. The jobs cross many different medical specialties and usually post compensation and experience levels.

Another key source for these types of jobs are the medical device headhunters or executive recruiters. Many medical device companies turn to independent recruiters to find candidates for them. These individuals are essentially sub contractors hired by a company that attempts to identify the right person for an open position. Ultimately, it is their job to connect the hiring company with a good candidate (or group of good candidates). If they are successful in doing so, they financially benefit from you being hired (via the hiring company).

If you can locate and convince the medical device headhunter that you are worthy of placement, you have yet another avenue to pursue the industry. Another great reason to use these individuals is that they sometimes know of opportunities before they are posted anywhere else. They are truly a great resource for those that know how to use them.

Finding a medical executive recruiter can be accomplished through a quick internet search. Once you identify a person or company, you want to sell your case and try to get them to recommend you for the opportunities that they may have or opportunities that they may encounter down the road.

The following chapter goes into more details about what not to tell medical device recruiters.

THREE THINGS TO NEVER TELL A RECRUITER

Have you ever submitted your application and never heard another word from the company that you applied to? The reality is that most applications disappear into what is commonly referred to as the "Black hole". What you need to do to circumvent this phenomenon is find a more effective approach to get your resume into the hands of the decision makers at the hiring companies.

We already discussed the value of medical recruiters or "Headhunters". As you recall, these are people that are specifically hired on the behalf of companies to find talented employment candidates. Finding a medical recruiter is the easy part. What you need to do next is know how to properly work with them for optimum results.

Recruiters act as your agent and yet another person helping you to obtain the position you desire. It should go without saying that you need to sell yourself to the recruiter so that they feel that you are worthy of their time. Once you have engaged a recruiter, there are a few things that you should do and a few things to avoid to help you achieve your desired result.

First, never tell a medical recruiter that you don't want to talk with them but instead you only want to talk directly with the company that is hiring. This is a good way to have yourself immediately excluded from consideration. These people are key gateways into some of these companies so you need to treat them as you would a direct employer. Remember, they are just as anxious to work with a well positioned candidate as you are to work with them. When you win, they win as your employment is their pay day.

Second, never tell a recruiter that you don't really care what type of medical device job you get and that you will take anything. This perceived sense of desperation and shows that you may be insincere about a job. It also demonstrates a lack of passion and poor judgment.

You need to be a little more specific in your desires. However, it is still acceptable and even advantageous to be a little vague. For instance, say that you want to work for a company in the medical device industry that has a good product and cares about its reputation. Or you want to work for a company that values people and wants to grow. Pretty much every company fits the above criteria and your wording is a much better reflection upon you.

Finally, never tell a recruiter that you don't have any experience! Just like with an employer, you need to tailor whatever experience you have into transferable, enticing and applicable experience. If you feel that whatever experience you have is inadequate, gain some sales experience as discussed previously, prior to speaking with the recruiters.

Recruiters can be one of the keys to your success but you must ensure that your interactions with them are positive. You need to be certain that you convince them that you are worth their time and investment so that they work their best to help you.

LESSON NINE: LOOKING THE PART

As you know, sales preparation is crucial in your career search. If you truly want to enter the medical device sales field, you have to make several investments. One of these investments is in you. It is well known that your appearance is a key element in this journey.

While all of these lessons are important, *looking the part* is a very crucial element in landing a job in this industry. You have to realize that medical device companies tend to put a strong emphasis on appearance. Medical device companies hire sales people that they think are going to represent their product well. In many ways, sales people are the outward symbol of the company. Like it or not, how you look can make or break your chances.

Did you know that over 60% of your first impression will come from appearance? It's true that vanity is important but the good news is that how you look and present yourself are more in your control that you probably think.

Spend a little time in the medical device world and you will find that most of the people are well put together. They are usually thin, very well groomed, well dressed and have a very successful look about them. Some will read this part and think that they are in big trouble as they do not think of themselves as attractive, but as I stated earlier, a good deal of your appearance is in your control.

You have to realize that very few people on this earth roll out of bed looking like a million bucks. It takes some work, it takes some knowledge and it takes some common sense. You can drastically influence your appearance if you just make take the time to invest in yourself and think about the impression you make on the outside world.

Since everyone is different, there is not an exact recipe that can be replicated time and time again. However, there are some universal tips that I can share with you that will help you get to where you are going.

I can't emphasize enough how important the look is for these companies. You need to make a solid investment here if you are serious about entering into the industry. While you may not agree with this the theory of judging a person by appearance, your appearance absolutely matters as you are ultimately the external representation of the company and the one that the customer will associate with the company. Rest assured that you don't have to be a Ralph Lauren model, but you need to have a nice, professional, and well put together look.

Tips for a great appearance:

1. Work out and eat right: It is rare to see notably overweight people in medical device sales. Generally speaking, the medical device sales people have an athletic appearance and are the proper weight for their height and frame. The best way to do this is through proper nutrition, regular aerobic activity, and mild weight resistance training.

2. Grooming: Proper grooming is necessary for many corporate positions but this is especially important in medical device sales. Women are usually in tune with grooming more than men so I am mainly speaking to the men on this point. You want to have a clean and professional appearance. Generally speaking, facial hair needs to be replaced with a clean shave, long hair needs to be cut and well groomed, your nails need to be trimmed, moisturize your face and pluck your eyebrows. A clean cut appearance is what you are after.

3. Jewelry: You are not in the business of selling jewelry so you should use it extremely sparingly. Men should never wear earrings or have any other visible piercings. You will want to be extremely conservative and keep the jewelry to an absolute minimum (wedding ring and watch). Women also need to be conservative in the amount and type of jewelry you wear. Be careful not to over accessorize.

4. Any tattoos that you may have should be fully covered at all times. Again, a clean conservative look is what these companies are after.

5. Make-Up: Ladies, don't go overboard with a lot of make-up. You want to look your best but you also want to look natural. A good habit is to choose lighter shades of lipstick, nail polish and eye liner that accentuates your appearance.

6. Perfume / Cologne: So many people go overboard with perfume / cologne and have no idea that they

are doing it. If you ever went shopping for a cologne or perfume, you probably picked up quite a few bottles and put them right back down because you didn't like the smell. Well guess what; due to personal preferences, there is a very good chance that the person sitting across the table from you might not like the scent that you prefer. Scent preferences are so specific that you are taking a gamble on the one that your wear. In the professional world it is best to keep the top on the perfume bottle or if you must put it on, apply very lightly.

7.   Dress for the Part: Companies assume that the way you look for an interview is the way you will look in front of their customers so appearance counts. The standard attire for medical device sales people are suits, ties (for men) and professional skirts or suits for women. For men, your suit needs to appear of decent quality, your shirt needs to be perfectly

pressed (and clean!), your tie needs to be conservative and your shoes need to be in good shape and shined. For women, be conservative in your appearance. A dark colored skirt or suit pants and a pressed dress shirt with moderate dress shoes is generally acceptable. Again, error on the side of being conservative.

8. Projecting Confidence: Looking the part means that you dress like a winner but you carry yourself like one too. This means standing up straight, holding your head up and projecting a sense that you are a winner that deserves the job. Walk, talk, and look confident.

You want your future employer to think that you are the perfect person to represent their product and they would be foolish if they didn't hire you. After all, they wouldn't want to lose such a great person to another company.

The key point is that you don't have to be the best looking person in the world but you need to do all the things to make the best impression possible. All of this is well within your control but it does mean an investment on your part.

It isn't always going to be easy to go to the gym or pass on the dessert or wear clothes that aren't always the most comfortable. However, these things are a part of your package and this package is being closely inspected when you venture into the interview process for a new job.

You may be tasked with selling millions of dollars worth of medical systems and so you need to look like you are worthy and capable of carrying such a responsibility. After all, there is a lot on the line for these companies and you need to inspire confidence in them so that they are comfortable with you.

LESSON TEN: INTERVIEWING FOR SUCCESS

When you get your opportunity to interview for a medical device sales position, you really have to make it count. We already covered some key points for the interview but the following are some other notable points to remember when interviewing with your potential future employer.

An interview is your first chance to sell in this industry. However, instead of selling a medical device product, you are selling yourself as their medical device salesperson. Consequently, you have to be confident in what you are saying. A good way to ensure your confidence is to practice your sales pitch. Rehearsal is the only way that you are going to optimize your performance in your interview and it is unquestionably time well spent.

Look at yourself, your experience, and your capabilities objectively and critically. If you do this exercise properly, you should be able to anticipate their objections before they even open their mouths. No matter how big or small, write each objection down on a piece of paper.

Now that you have a list of probable objections, you need to think about answers to overcome each one of their reservations. No matter if it is lack of experience, a gap in employment or anything else, you need to have your strategy down before walking into the interview. Come up with a sound answer for each objection and practice your response until it feels convincing and natural.

Next, find a way to put yourself in their shoes. Think about what is important to them and what they are looking for in an applicant. Then find a way to be that applicant!

The fact is that employers have many candidates to choose from these days. With so many choices, they are trying to find ways to eliminate some applicants and bring their options down to a manageable number. Don't let yourself be eliminated by lack of preparation. Do the up front preparation and then execute your strategy with precision to ensure that you are last person standing.

Another thing to remember is a differentiation technique. Have you ever been to a seminar or meeting where at the end everything and everyone just blurred together. You may have spent hours there but nothing really stood out and captured a place in your memory. The same thing happens during the interview process; interviewees and answers tend to blend together and candidates start to look the same. You need to find ways to differentiate yourself to make a lasting impression.

Besides being the most prepared candidate, perhaps you will be the most energetic. Or perhaps you will share the most intriguing success story. Or maybe you are the most polished candidate of the group. Or perhaps you left your future employer with the most impressive accomplishment packet or had the most impressive award list.

You have to remember that you are not the only person interviewing so consider how you will make a lasting impression. The better the impression, the better your chances of reaching your goal.

Finally, remember the courtesy follow-up after the interview. The employees from these companies took time out of their busy day to interview you and it is important (and expected) to thank them for their time. A nice benefit is at the same time you can also remind them of your accomplishments and why you think you are the perfect fit for the job.

SUMMARY

It is important to note that a key element to this equation is persistence. When I began my initial job search, I didn't have a book like ***How to get a medical device sales job*** to turn to and learn from. Consequently, I had to figure all of this out myself making it a lot harder for me to land that first job. However, I never gave up as I knew that my persistence would pay off.

I learned from experience and I applied all of the principles and techniques that we have been discussing until I landed the job I wanted. I then took my inside knowledge of the business and refined the concepts even further. All of this means that you can bypass the challenges that will pose many others that are considering this job and accelerate your path to success.

Be forewarned, you will most likely face challenges and you may not get the dream job on the first try but the key is to stay focused on your goal and stay committed. You can do it if you truly put your mind and energy to it and I can tell you from experience that it is unquestionably worth the effort.

The future of the medical device sales industry is very bright as both medicine and technology are constantly advancing. The demographics are also very good for this business which keeps a steady supply of patients that will need the technology that you are selling.

Irrespective of the economy, jobs in medical device sales will continue to remain strong due to the constant need for the technology and products. The great news is that where there is a need for products, there is a need for medical device sales representatives to sell these products.

Entering the world of medical device sales is worth the investment and you can do it! Apply these lessons, be passionate and don't give up until you have achieved your goal.

Best of luck in your endeavor and enjoy your new career!

ABOUT THE AUTHOR

My name is Daniel Riley and I wrote this book to help people like you obtain what I believe to be one of the greatest jobs in business. The tips described in this book do work and have helped many people like you reach their dream.

I have had a lot of fun over the years in this business and hope that you enjoy it as much as I have.

45045728R00046

Made in the USA
San Bernardino, CA
30 January 2017